TAKE A SEAT—MAKE A STAND

TAKE A SEAT—MAKE A STAND

A HERO IN THE FAMILY

The Story Of Sarah Keys Evans, A Civil Rights Hero Who Would Not Be Moved

Amy Nathan
Author of the 2005 nonfiction Clarion Award Winner:
COUNT ON US

iUniverse, Inc.
New York Lincoln Shanghai

TAKE A SEAT—MAKE A STAND
A HERO IN THE FAMILY

iUniverse books may be ordered through booksellers or by contacting:

iUniverse
2021 Pine Lake Road, Suite 100
Lincoln, NE 68512
www.iuniverse.com
1-800-Authors (1-800-288-4677)

The views expressed in this work are solely those of the author and do not necessarily reflect the views of the publisher, and the publisher hereby disclaims any responsibility for them.

Photo Credits
All images in the book and on the cover are courtesy of Sarah Keys Evans except for the following:
photos of Krystal Hargrave by herself, with her grandmother, and with her parents, are courtesy of Bradley Hargrave and Cornelia Hargrave; photos of Dovey Roundtree and of Korean War soldiers are courtesy of the National Archives; photo of the Carolina Coach bus is courtesy of the Library of Congress; photo of Sarah Keys Evans at the Women In Military Service For America Memorial is courtesy of the Women in Military Service For America Memorial Foundation, Inc. The final two photos of Sarah Keys Evans in the book were taken by the author, © 2006 Amy Nathan.

ISBN-13: 978-0-595-41761-2 (pbk)
ISBN-13: 978-0-595-86102-6 (ebk)
ISBN-10: 0-595-41761-2 (pbk)
ISBN-10: 0-595-86102-4 (ebk)

Printed in the United States of America

Dedicated to Sarah Keys Evans
and also
to her father, David A. Keys, Sr., (1896–1980), of whom she said:
"He was the guiding force behind my quest for justice."

Contents

Acknowledgments

I am grateful to Sarah Keys Evans for sharing her memories with me, and for having had the courage to help change things for the better in this country. She kindly put me in touch with other members of her family, which is how I was able to speak with her teen-aged niece, Krystal Hargrave.

I would like to thank Krystal for telling me about the hero project she did when she was in fifth grade. How wonderful that she asked her grandmother for help with that project and that her grandmother suggested that Krystal write about Aunt Sarah. That is actually when Krystal first learned about her Aunt Sarah's contribution to Civil Rights history.

Thanks also go to Krystal's grandmother, Cornelia Keys Hargrave, for speaking with me about her memories and also about her feelings concerning the impact on the family of her older sister Sarah's ICC case. I'm also grateful to Krystal's parents, Bradley and Teresa Hargrave, for sharing their memories and photos; to Sarah's brother William Keys for allowing photos of him as a child to be shown in the book; and to two of Sarah Keys Evans's other nieces—Joan Dudley Parker and Julie Anne Waters Graves—for speaking with me about their memories of Aunt Sarah.

I am also extremely grateful to Brigadier General Wilma L. Vaught, USAF (Retired), the President of the Women In Military Service For America Memorial Foundation, Inc., both for honoring Mrs. Evans with an exhibit at the Memorial and also for contributing the eloquent statement that appears on this book's cover.

In addition, I would also like to thank the following: Dr. Judith Bellafaire, Britta Granrud, Linda Witt, and Marilla S. Cushman of the Women In Military Service For America Memorial Foundation, Inc., for putting me in touch with Sarah Keys Evans, providing valuable background information, photographs, and encouragement; Constance A. Burns, for helping to spread the word about this project; Professor Carol Buckler, for tracking down important legal information on the ICC case; Professor Henry Louis Gates, Jr., for his encouragement and suggestions; my brother, Rock Singewald, and his friend Anne Raver for believing in this project; and the wonderful students at my alma mater, Western High School in Baltimore, Maryland, for responding so enthusiastically when I told them about Sarah Keys Evans and her struggle for justice at the school's 2006 Unity Day celebration, a response that encouraged me to press forward with this book project.

There is, of course, one more person to thank, the one without whom this book would never have been possible: its cheerleader-in-chief, my husband, Carl Nathan, whose constant encouragement, thoughtful suggestions, and generous financial contribution enabled this book to go from idea to reality.

Krystal

Grandma

Aunt Sarah

Chapter 1: A Hero in the Family

"Yum, apple pie," said Krystal, as she plopped her school books on the kitchen table. "Can I have some?"

"Not now," said her mother. "It's for tonight. We're having dinner at Grandma and Grandpa's house. I promised to bring a pie for dessert."

"Oh yeah, that's right," said Krystal.

"Do you have much homework to do this weekend?" asked her mom.

"Just that hero project," said Krystal.

"Have you chosen someone to write about?" asked her mom.

"No, I can't decide," said Krystal. "The project is due on Monday! I don't know what to do. How am I going to pick someone to write about?"

"Ask Grandma tonight," said Krystal's mom. "She was a teacher, you know, before she retired. She'll have lots of great ideas for you."

Grandma and Krystal

That evening at dinner, Krystal sat next to her grandmother. Right before dessert, Krystal tapped her grandmother on the shoulder and whispered, "Can I ask you a question?"

"Sure, honey, what is it?" answered Grandma.

"I need to find a hero to write about," said Krystal. "It's for a project in school. I don't know who to pick."

"That sounds like an interesting project," said Grandma. "Does your hero have to be somebody you're studying about in school?"

"No, it can be anybody," said Krystal. "It just has to be somebody we look up to, somebody who inspires us."

"Well, I know who I'd pick," said Grandma. "We have a hero right here in the family—my older sister Sarah, your great aunt."

"Aunt Sarah?" said Krystal.

"I know you don't get to see her much, what with you living in New Jersey and she's way over in Brooklyn," said Grandma. "But you remember your Aunt Sarah, don't you?"

"Sure," said Krystal.

"She's been my hero ever since I was a teen-ager," said Grandma. "She isn't the kind of person you might expect to be a hero. She was always very shy and quiet. But shy people can be heroes, too."

"They sure can," added Grandpa, who had been listening in on the conversation. "Sarah was shy, but she was brave, too."

"What did she do?" asked Krystal.

"Well, you know about Rosa Parks, don't you—the woman who refused to move to the back of a bus?" asked Grandma.

"Sure," said Krystal. "We learned about Rosa Parks in school. She helped fight discrimination."

"So did your Aunt Sarah," said Grandma. "Sarah did exactly what Rosa Parks did, only Sarah did it three years *before* Rosa Parks!"

"Wow," said Krystal.

"Your Aunt Sarah was only twenty-two years old at the time," said Grandma. "It was late at night, on a hot summer night in 1952, at a lonely bus station in North Carolina."

"Sounds scary," said Krystal.

"Yes, it was," said Grandma. "Sarah was very brave that night and kept on being brave, standing up for her rights. Sarah ended up making things better in this country for everyone."

"How did she do that?" asked Krystal.

"Let me get my old photo album," said Grandma. "Then let's go into the living room. We can enjoy your mother's delicious apple pie in there while I tell you all about it."

The whole family gathered in the living room to have some pie—and hear about Aunt Sarah.

"Look, here's an old photo of Sarah," said Grandma, opening the photo album. "It was taken at our home in North Carolina that summer when her adventure began."

Krystal sat close to Grandma so she could have a good look at the photos.

Sarah at home in North Carolina, August 1952.

"And here's a photo of me with Sarah a few years later, looking at some beautiful flowering bushes at a park in Brooklyn, New York. That's where Sarah was living by then," said Grandma.

"Connie, you and Sarah look so young and pretty in that photo," said Grandpa.

"Oh, enough of that," said Grandma. "Now, let me get started with the story. Krystal, your father knows about it, too. Maybe he can help me with some of the details."

"I'd be glad to," said Krystal's dad. "I remember you telling me about Aunt Sarah when I was a kid, just about Krystal's age."

So together, Grandma and Krystal's dad described how Aunt Sarah became a hero so many years ago. Here's the tale they told.

Connie (Grandma) and Sarah (right) in Brooklyn, New York, in 1955.

Sarah's high school graduation picture, 1948.

Chapter 2: Growing Up

First, Grandma paused to make sure Krystal understood how different things were for African Americans back in 1952, especially in the South where Grandma and Aunt Sarah grew up. There were seven kids in the family: Connie (that's Grandma), Sarah, Marie, Angela, David, Jim, and William. They lived on a farm with their mother and father—David and Vivian Keys—in the town of Washington, North Carolina. The part of town where they lived was called Keysville, named after some of their ancestors.

At that time, many white Southerners were prejudiced against African Americans.

White officials in states like North Carolina made unfair laws called "Jim Crow" laws to keep blacks and whites from having much to do with each other. One of those laws kept black kids from going to public school with white kids.

Grandma explained that her father wanted his kids to get a good education. So Grandma and Sarah attended a school that was run by the Catholic church. It was only for black kids, but it was a very good school and the kids learned a lot.

There were also all kinds of other things black people weren't allowed to do back then down South. At movie theaters, blacks had to sit upstairs in the balcony, instead of downstairs in the better seats, which were only for whites. Many restaurants were only for white people. Even some churches were only for whites and refused to let in black people.

Of course, some white Southerners got along well with black peo-ple and thought it was terrible that blacks were treated so badly. But for a long time, speaking up in the South against this unfair treat-ment was dangerous, whether you were white or black. People who spoke up were often beaten. Sometimes black people were put in jail and even killed for crimes they didn't do. Times were tough.

Grandma went on to explain that Sarah left her North Carolina hometown right after graduating from high school. She moved up North where she hoped things would be better. For a while, Sarah attended nursing school in New Jersey and then she worked in an office in New York City.

*Sarah (left) with older sister Marie
in New York, soon after Sarah
moved up North.*

After working in that office in New York City for a while, Sarah decided to join the Army. She became a WAC—a member of the Women's Army Corps. That's what the women's part of the Army was called back then.

Joining the Army might seem like an unusual thing for a shy and quiet young woman to do. But Sarah thought being in the Army would open up a lot of opportunities. It would give her a chance to learn new things, meet new people, visit new places, while also serving her country.

Blacks and whites worked together in the Army. Sarah liked that. Plus, she thought that being in the Women's Army Corps might help her stop being so shy.

Sarah (center) with two friends she made during WAC Basic Training.

Army life could be hard at times, especially all the marching and tough physical exercises that new soldiers have to do as part of Basic Training. But Sarah was proud of how well she handled each new challenge she faced as a WAC. After she completed Basic Training, the Army sent her to work as a receptionist at a hospital on an Army base up North in Fort Dix, New Jersey.

She was becoming more self-confident, more sure of herself. She was slowly losing some of the shyness she had as a girl growing up in the South.

She would need all her new self-confidence to handle the trouble she would face on that hot summer night in 1952, at a lonely North Carolina bus stop.

*Sarah in her Women's Army
Corps uniform.*

Chapter 3: Taking a Seat

On that hot August night in 1952, Sarah was on a bus that was making its way to North Carolina. She was traveling from her New Jersey Army base in order to go down to North Carolina for a short vacation at home with her family. It was her first trip home since joining the Army about a year before.

She was proudly wearing her Army uniform. Military people were supposed to wear their uniforms when they traveled.

She was eager to see her mom, dad, her younger sisters, and her little brother. She wanted to tell them all about her Army experiences.

Sarah's brother Jim Keys was in the Air Force and served in Korea during the Korean War.

Sarah's brother David Keys was in the Army and he also served in Korea during the Korean War.

She was sad that two of her brothers, Jim and David, wouldn't be there to greet her when she got home. They were in the military, too. They were far from home, serving in Korea, where the U.S. was fighting a war.

American soldiers serving in the Korean War.

The bus ride to North Carolina took many hours. She had climbed on board early in the morning in New Jersey, near her Army base.

She sat in a seat toward the middle of the bus. She always found that to be the most comfortable place to sit on a bus. She slept through most of the trip, snuggled down in her seat as the bus rumbled along.

After midnight, the bus reached its first stop in North Carolina, in a town called Roanoke Rapids. Sarah was still asleep. This stop was in the northern part of the state. Her hometown was farther south. The bus would make many more stops before reaching her hometown. She figured she didn't need to wake up yet.

A new driver took over the bus at this first stop in North Carolina. The bus was very crowded. There were other military people on board who, like Sarah, were also in their uniforms. A young white man, a Marine, was sitting next to her.

The new bus driver walked down the aisle of the bus, checking people's tickets.

When he saw Sarah, he stopped.

"Move to the back of the bus," he said to Sarah.

Sarah

Sarah raised her head, slowly waking up.

"I'm comfortable right here," said Sarah.

She saw that the driver was checking people's tickets. So she reached over the Marine who was next to her in order to show the driver her ticket.

"I'm not taking your ticket," the driver said.

He sounded angry.

Sarah didn't know why.

Then the bus driver said everyone had to get off the bus and climb onto another bus.

"Everyone except that woman who refused to move," he said. "She can sit here until this bus moves out, but it's not going any place tonight."

A bus something like the one Sarah took. This photo was taken in North Carolina a few years before Sarah's trip.

Chapter 4: Big Trouble

Sarah didn't understand what the bus driver meant about the bus not going anywhere that night. So she got off the bus, too. The Marine sitting next to her quickly left the bus. A white sailor who was standing helped her with her luggage. Sarah stood in line with all the other passengers waiting to get on the new bus.

But the driver wouldn't let her on the new bus.

She thought maybe something was wrong with her ticket. She walked over to the small station house that was nearby. She went inside and walked up to the ticket window.

But as soon as Sarah walked up, the ticket seller closed the ticket window and wouldn't help Sarah.

A tall black man was sweeping the floor inside the station house. He said to Sarah, "Miss, don't you know where you are?"

The look on his face made Sarah realize suddenly that she was in big trouble.

She walked out of the station house and went over to the passengers waiting to get on the new bus.

"You're not riding this bus tonight," the driver said firmly to Sarah.

Suddenly, she turned around. There were three white policemen.

"Is this the one?" asked one policeman, pointing toward Sarah.

"Yes," said the bus driver.

A policeman put his hand on Sarah's shoulder.

"You're coming with us," he said. He led Sarah to a police car and made her get inside.

"Where are you taking me?" Sarah asked the policemen.

"We're taking you to jail," one of the officers said.

"Why?" she asked.

"We can get you for disorderly conduct," he said.

"But nothing happened," she said.

"We don't even have to get you all the way to jail," he said.

Then she became very scared.

She had heard stories of police officers in the South beating up black people—and even killing them—on the way to jail.

Luckily, these police officers didn't harm her during the ride. Before long they arrived at the jail.

She asked if she could call her family. The policemen said they would call her family for her. But they never did.

They locked her up in a jail cell. It had only a dirty mattress on the floor and a small sink. She was all alone in there.

She spent the rest of the night and the next morning in that cell, all by herself, walking back and forth.

She was too scared to sleep.

She cried.

She prayed.

She knew she had to keep strong so she could think clearly when the police officers came to get her. She didn't know what they might try to do to her.

Sarah in her WAC uniform.

The next day, just before noon, she was brought before the town's chief of police.

"What kind of outfit is that you're wearing?" asked the police chief.

"This is a United States Army uniform," she said. "I'm in the Women's Army Corps."

That seemed to make him angry.

He told her she could go if she paid a fine of $25. Money was worth more back then. That would be like having to pay $190 today. Luckily, Sarah had enough money to pay the fine. Otherwise, who knows what might have happened to her.

Then, other officers took her back to the bus station. They put her on another bus that was heading down to her hometown. The officers took her to a seat in the back of the bus. They told her she had to sit there. She decided it was best to stay in that seat for the rest of her trip home.

Why did the policemen arrest Sarah?

Back then, there were Jim Crow laws in many Southern states that said blacks could sit only in seats at the back of a bus. Sitting back there was usually much hotter than sitting near the front of a bus. That's because the engine was located at the back of a bus and gave off hot, nasty fumes. Sitting in the back also meant you usually had a more bumpy ride. The more comfortable seats were toward the front of a bus. Those seats were for whites.

Sarah knew about those Jim Crow laws.

But she also knew that six years earlier, in 1946, the United States Supreme Court had said those laws couldn't be used on bus trips like the one Sarah was taking: *trips that went from one state to another state.*

The Supreme Court in its 1946 ruling had said that black people could sit wherever they wanted when traveling from *state-to-state*, as Sarah was doing.

According to the Supreme Court, a state could make laws *only* for people traveling *inside* that particular state. So if North Carolina had a bus seat law, that North Carolina law could be used *only* for people traveling *inside* North Carolina. However, North Carolina's law couldn't be used for bus trips that started in another state and then came into North Carolina.

Sarah's father, David Keys, had read a newspaper article about that 1946 Supreme Court decision. He had told Sarah about it before she left home.

So she sat in the middle of the bus. After all, she was definitely on a state-to-state trip. Her bus passed through *five* states before reaching North Carolina.

However, some bus companies in the South found a sneaky way to get around the Supreme Court.

In its 1946 decision, the Supreme Court had talked only about *laws* that a state might make.

It hadn't said anything about *rules* that a bus company might make.

Some bus companies in the South made their *own rules* about where people could sit, even on state-to-state trips.

Not all bus drivers made people obey those rules.

Unfortunately, Sarah ran into a bus driver who decided to enforce his company's unfair rules. She was arrested because she refused to obey that driver when he told her to move to the back of the bus.

However, thanks to what Sarah soon would do, bus companies would no longer be able to make up rules that would force people to sit in certain seats just because of the color of their skin.

Sarah's mother, Vivian Keys, and her father, David Keys,
during the summer of 1952.

Chapter 5: Making a Stand

When Sarah reached her home, she told her parents what had happened.

Her father became angry.

It was insulting that someone could be treated like a second-class citizen that way. It was especially unfair because Sarah was being a very responsible citizen, serving her country during wartime, as a member of the Women's Army Corps. Her two brothers were also doing their part for their country, risking their lives fighting in Korea.

Sarah's father had put up with a lot of discrimination in his years of living in the South. He had tried his best to protect his kids from the unfair treatment that was all around them. Now trouble had found its way into his family.

This latest insult was just too much. He was determined to do something about it. So was Sarah.

Sarah's mother, younger brother William, and father at home in North Carolina.

Sarah's father knew that change was coming. He worked on construction projects, as a cement mason, helping to build new buildings. Sometimes he worked in North Carolina. But often he worked up in the nation's capital, Washington, D.C., constructing buildings there. He liked to read newspapers, to learn what was happening in other parts of the U.S. He knew that there were people who were trying to change things for the better for black people.

He was glad to know that Sarah was ready to do her part to help bring about these changes.

So Sarah and her father went back to the small town of Roanoke Rapids, North Carolina, where she had been arrested. It took a lot of courage for Sarah to go back to that town. There was no telling what officials there might do to her if she came back.

She and her father arranged to meet a lawyer in Roanoke Rapids. The lawyer lived in North Carolina and said he would try to help. But there wasn't much he could do. They spoke with town officials and tried to persuade them that Sarah had done nothing wrong and should not have been arrested. But the officials wouldn't change their minds.

Sarah and her father tried one more time, going back to this town on yet another day, but they couldn't change any minds that day, either.

That didn't stop Sarah and her father.

They were definitely not going to give up.

A friend put her father in contact with another lawyer who might know more about how to handle a case like this. This lawyer was a young black woman named Dovey Roundtree. She worked in Washington, D.C., had just finished law school, and was interested in trying to improve things for black people.

While in law school, Mrs. Roundtree helped other lawyers prepare for a big case that would soon be heading to the Supreme Court. That case aimed to put an end to discrimination against blacks in the nation's public schools.

Now that she was out of law school, Mrs. Roundtree had set up her own law firm with another black lawyer, Julius Robertson.

Sarah's father telephoned Mrs. Roundtree.

Would Mrs. Roundtree and her partner be interested in taking on Sarah's case? You bet!

Dovey Roundtree when she was in the Army as a WAC during World War II.

Sarah and her father traveled to Washington, D.C., to meet with Mrs. Roundtree.

Sarah started to feel shy again—and a little scared.

This was the first time she had been in a lawyer's office. It was also the first time she had ever met a woman lawyer.

But Sarah soon learned that she and Mrs. Roundtree had something in common: the Women's Army Corps. For several years, during the last war—World War II—Mrs. Roundtree had served in the Women's Army Corps. That helped Sarah feel more comfortable, knowing she was talking with someone who had been a soldier just like her.

Soon she was telling Mrs. Roundtree all about what had happened.

Mrs. Roundtree thought Sarah should take legal action against the bus company. Sarah and her father agreed. Mrs. Roundtree said she would handle all the details. Sarah headed back to the Army base in New Jersey where she was stationed.

Sarah

Chapter 6: Testifying

At first, Sarah didn't tell her Army friends about what had happened on the bus. She didn't know what people would think if they heard she had been arrested. But after a while, she told the two women who were her best friends in the Army: one was black and the other white. Both thought it was terrible that Sarah had been treated so badly.

That helped Sarah feel better.

But deep inside, she still felt upset by what had happened. She didn't share these feelings with many people. Instead she kept busy doing a good job in the Army.

Every once in a while, Sarah would hear from Mrs. Roundtree about how things were going on the case. At first, Mrs. Roundtree tried to sue the bus company in a court in Washington, D.C. That court case didn't work out so well.

Mrs. Roundtree didn't give up easily. She decided to present Sarah's situation to the government office that was supposed to keep an eye on the nation's bus and train companies. This office was called the Interstate Commerce Commission, or ICC, for short.

Mrs. Roundtree decided to file a formal complaint with the ICC against the bus company that had mistreated Sarah.

Legal cases have names, usually the names of the people or companies involved. Sarah's complaint before the ICC had her name on it. It was called:

Sarah Keys v. Carolina Coach Company.

The "v." stands for a Latin word "versus" which means "against."

A Carolina Coach Company bus.

Legal work tends to go slowly.

It takes a long time to prepare a complaint to send to an agency like the ICC.

A little over a year after Sarah had been arrested, Mrs. Roundtree finally finished up all the work on the complaint about Sarah's situation and sent it to the ICC.

Then the ICC took its time deciding what it would do about Sarah's case.

Sarah just had to be patient and wait.

Soon Sarah's two-year tour of duty in the Army came to an end. She decided not to join up again, but to try something new.

She left the Army in October 1953. The military gives money to its former soldiers after they leave the service, to help them pay for schooling. Mrs. Roundtree had used the money she received from the Army to go to law school. Sarah used the money she received to go to a different kind of school so she could learn how to do something she had always been interested in: being a hair stylist. For a year, she went to beauty school at night while working full time during the day as a clerk in an office in New York City.

In the spring of 1954, Sarah received a phone call from Mrs. Roundtree. The ICC was ready finally to consider Sarah's case. Sarah would have to travel down to Washington, D.C., to testify— tell her story to the members of the ICC.

Sarah started to feel scared again.

She was nervous about talking to such important government officials. She had never done anything like that before.

She talked with her father on the phone. He told her that there were always choices to make in life. If she didn't want to testify, that was one choice she had. But if she decided to go ahead and testify, he would be there in Washington to help her.

Her father said that he would bring along William, her eleven-year-old brother. They would sit in the audience in the big room where the ICC had its meetings.

Knowing that they would be there made Sarah feel better.

She decided to go to Washington, D.C.

She took a train this time, not a bus.

Sarah with younger brother William.

The ICC meeting in Washington took place on May 12, 1954. It was almost like a trial. Different lawyers asked Sarah questions.

Sarah was asked to speak louder because she had such a soft, quiet voice.

The lawyer for the bus company was very tough. He asked question after question. It seemed like he was trying to make Sarah change her story. But Sarah didn't let the lawyer bother her. She told the truth about what had happened on that hot summer night at that bus stop in North Carolina.

Finally the questioning stopped.

The ICC didn't take long to reach a decision.

Sadly, the ICC said there was nothing wrong with making black people sit in the back of a bus.

Sarah had lost!

She was shocked!

And disappointed.

So were her father and brother.

So was Mrs. Roundtree.

But they weren't ready to give up.

They were determined to keep trying.

Sarah took a train back to New York.

Mrs. Roundtree got busy trying to figure out what to do next.

Sarah in 1955.

Chapter 7: Making a Difference

It turned out that there were eleven members of the ICC, but the decision in Sarah's case had been made by only *one* of those ICC members.

Mrs. Roundtree thought that wasn't fair. She decided to go back to the ICC and try to make *all* its members consider Sarah's complaint. New York Congressman Adam Clayton Powell, Jr., agreed. He helped persuade the ICC to reconsider its decision.

So the ICC decided that *all* its members would indeed take a second look at Sarah's case.

That meant Sarah had to do some more waiting. She hoped things would turn out better the second time around.

Sarah knew that another important Civil Rights case was also being considered in Washington. It was the one on schools that Mrs. Roundtree had helped do research for when she was in law school. This case was called *Brown v. Board of Education*. It was being considered by the U.S. Supreme Court.

On May 17, 1954, the Supreme Court reached a decision in that school case. The Supreme Court ordered that black children could no longer be forced to go to separate all-black schools. From then on, public schools in the U.S. had to be integrated, with blacks and whites being able to attend school together.

Sarah hoped that this Supreme Court decision would help the ICC realize that discrimination on bus rides had to end, too.

Meanwhile, a big Civil Rights group, the NAACP (National Association for the Advancement of Colored People), had also filed a complaint with the ICC about discrimination on trains. The head of the U.S. Department of Justice, Attorney General Herbert Brownell, tried to help the NAACP's case. He sent a message to the ICC to say that he agreed with the NAACP, that it was time to end discrimination in state-to-state travel. Maybe that would help Sarah's case, too.

Finally, on the morning of November 25, 1955, Sarah received the phone call she had been waiting so long for.

She had graduated from beauty school by then and was working at a New York beauty salon as a hair stylist and beauty consultant.

The phone call was from Mrs. Roundtree.

The ICC had reached a new decision.

This time Sarah won!

A majority of the ICC members had decided that it was wrong for people on state-to-state trips to be forced to sit in certain seats on a bus because of the color of their skin.

Not only did the ICC decide it was wrong to force black people to sit in certain seats. It was also against the law!

There was a U.S. law called the Interstate Commerce Act which said that people on state-to-state trips should not be forced to experience any "prejudice or disadvantage in any respect whatsoever." The ICC members decided that forcing people to sit in certain seats because of their race showed both "prejudice" and "disadvantage." So those unfair seating rules broke that U.S. law. Rules like that would not be allowed any longer.

Here is the concluding paragraph of the actual ICC decision.

We find that the practice of defendant requiring that Negro interstate passengers occupy space or seats in specified portions of its buses, subjects such passengers to unjust discrimination, and undue and unreasonable prejudice and disadvantage, in violation of section 216 (d) of the act, and is therefore unlawful.

An order will be entered prohibiting the continuation of such practice.

Here is the first page of the ICC decision.

No. MC–C–1564

SARAH KEYS v. CAROLINA COACH COMPANY

Decided November 7, 1955

Upon complaint, defendant found to be engaged in certain practices subjecting Negro passengers to unjust discrimination and unreasonable prejudice and disadvantage, in violation of section 216 (d) of the Interstate Commerce Act. Order entered requiring defendant to cease and desist from such practices.

Julius W. Robertson, Dovey J. Roundtree, and *Frank D. Reeves* for complainant.

Frank F. Roberson for defendant.

REPORT OF THE COMMISSION

BY THE COMMISSION:

Exceptions were filed by complainant to the order recommended by the examiner, and the defendant replied. The parties have been heard in oral argument. Our conclusions differ from those recommended.

By a complaint filed on September 1, 1953, Sarah Keys, of New York, N. Y., alleges that the Carolina Coach Company, a corporation, of Raleigh, N. C., a motor common carrier of passengers, has subjected her to unjust discrimination and undue and unreasonable prejudice and disadvantage, contrary to the provisions of the Interstate Commerce Act, in that on or about August 2, 1952, while a passenger on one of the defendant's buses, she was, at Roanoke Rapids, N. C., refused further passage and subjected by defendant's employees to false arrest and imprisonment solely because of her race and color. An order is sought requiring the defendant to cease and desist and refrain from the alleged acts of discrimination and prejudice. As filed, the complaint also included a request for monetary damages, but that portion of the complaint was dismissed by order entered February 24, 1954, because of our lack of power to award damages for violations of part II of the act.

The circumstances giving rise to the filing of the complaint are fairly clear. On August 1, 1952, complainant, a Negro, who was at that time a member of the Women's Army Corps stationed at Fort Dix, N. J., purchased a bus ticket from Safeway Trails, Inc., a motor common carrier of passengers, for transportation from Trenton, N. J., to Washington, N. C. A joint-line ticket was issued for transportation over the lines of three carriers, namely, Safeway Trails, Inc.,

64 M. C. C.

This ICC decision went farther than the Supreme Court's ruling of a few years before. That earlier 1946 Supreme Court ruling had outlawed only unfair *laws* that a state might make—not *rules* that a bus company might make.

This new ICC decision covered state laws, company rules, and anything else anyone might think up as a way to force black people to sit in certain seats while traveling from state-to-state.

That same day, the ICC announced a similar decision in the NAACP train case. As far as state-to-state trips were concerned, from then on it would be illegal for anybody to make people sit in certain seats on a bus or a train just because of their race.

Tribune City Edition

FIVE CENTS

Segregation's End On Buses, Trains Ordered by I. C. C.

Newspaper headline November 26, 1955.

Sarah was so happy. She told the people in the beauty salon about the ICC decision. They were amazed.

She called her family to tell them the good news.

But she didn't have much time to talk to them.

Soon the beauty salon was filled with television reporters and newspaper reporters.

Other reporters called on the phone. They all wanted to talk with the brave young woman who had the courage to stand up for her rights and the rights of all people of color in this country.

The next day there were articles about her great victory in newspapers all across the U.S.

A reporter named Max Lerner was so happy about Sarah's ICC ruling that he wrote in a big New York City newspaper, the *New York Post*: "I light a candle in my heart with the knowledge that, white and black alike, we can now ride together."

Krystal's dad, Krystal, her little sister Alexis,
her brother Bradley, and Krystal's mother.

Chapter 8: "Never Give Up"

"Wow!" said Krystal when she heard what Aunt Sarah had done. Krystal knew she had found the best possible hero for her school project.

"So from then on, could everybody sit anywhere they wanted to on a bus or train?" asked Krystal.

"On most state-to-state trips," said Grandma. "Most bus and train companies changed their ways."

"But a few companies didn't obey the ICC," said Krystal's dad. "In some parts of the deep South, blacks still had to sit in the back of the bus, even if they were traveling from state-to-state. And, of course, things were also bad if you took a *local* bus ride *inside* a Southern state. To get all bus companies everywhere to change their ways took a lot of people marching in the streets and having protests."

"Yes, just one week after we heard of Sarah's victory, and after all those newspapers all over the country wrote about her, Rosa Parks did what Sarah had done," said Grandma. "Rosa Parks refused to move to the back of a *local* bus in Montgomery, Alabama—not a state-to-state bus like the one Sarah had been on. Rosa Parks got arrested. There were all kinds of protests and demonstrations down there, led by someone else you probably know of, the Reverend Martin Luther King, Jr."

"That's right," said Krystal's dad. "That's when Dr. King got started as a Civil Rights leader. After those protests down in Alabama, the U.S. Supreme Court said bus companies couldn't make blacks sit in the back of a bus on *local* trips either."

"So that's when everybody could sit anywhere they wanted?" asked Krystal.

"Not exactly," said Grandma. "Some places in the deep South *still* refused to obey the law. It took even more protests all over the South a few years later, with sit-ins and also something called the Freedom Rides. Then, finally, in the early 1960s, the U.S. government forced *all* bus companies, no matter where they were, to do what the ICC had said they had to do back in 1955, with your Aunt Sarah's case."

"Then finally everybody on any bus could sit anywhere they wanted," said Grandpa. "Some blacks had a difficult time at first trusting the new ruling, that it really would be OK to sit anywhere on a bus. But many others took advantage of their new freedoms."

"Thank goodness there isn't that kind of discrimination any more," said Krystal's mom.

"Your Aunt Sarah really helped move things along," said Grandma. "There's even an exhibit that tells about her at the Women's Memorial in Washington, D.C."

"She really is a hero," said Krystal.

"Yes, she is," said Grandma. "You know, when she was arrested, I was only seventeen years old. I would be going away to college before too long, to become a teacher. I was scared the same thing might happen to me. But your Aunt Sarah's courage made me a stronger person. If she could stand up to something she thought was wrong, then I could, too. She set a good example for me to follow — and maybe for you to follow, too."

A few days later, Krystal's dad called Aunt Sarah to tell her about Krystal's school project.

Aunt Sarah was so pleased that Krystal had written about her.

"I'd like to see that report some day," said Aunt Sarah.

"Next time you come over to visit, we'll be sure to show it to you," he said.

That summer, Aunt Sarah came to Krystal's house for a big family picnic. She gave Krystal a special hug.

"Thank you for writing about me for school," said Aunt Sarah.

"The teacher and the other kids were really interested," said Krystal. "It was so great that you stood up for your rights. How did you have the courage to do that?"

"You have to be strong and remember that there's always that right person out there to help you," said Aunt Sarah. "It might be someone in your family. Or your family can tell you who can help. I had my father to help me, and then he found out who could help him to help me. As long as I had my father, I would never give up."

"Did you ever get discouraged?" asked Krystal.

"When I did, I would just try to put those thoughts out of my head," said Aunt Sarah. "I'm glad I didn't give up. I'm glad I was able to help unlock another door of freedom."

"I'm glad I have a hero in my family," said Krystal.

Krystal and her Aunt Sarah.

Sarah in 1999 at the dedication of an exhibit about her at the Women In Military Service For America Memorial, which is located at the entrance to Arlington National Cemetery, just outside of Washington, D.C.

Epilogue:
Author's Note and Historical Overview

I first learned of Sarah Keys Evans in 2001 when I was working on my book for young people on the history of women in the military— COUNT ON US—and was doing research at the Women In Military Service For America Memorial. I noticed a small exhibit that described the role Mrs. Evans played in the Civil Rights Movement. I was surprised that I had never heard of her, even though I had been a history major in college and had read a great deal about the Civil Rights era. I was determined to find out more. The historian at the Women In Military Service For America Memorial Foundation put me in touch with Mrs. Evans. I've had many wonderful conversations since, with Mrs. Evans and members of her family. The more I learned, the more amazed I was by what she had accomplished as a young woman working with another young woman, her lawyer Dovey Roundtree.

I was intrigued to hear that Mrs. Evans's niece, Krystal Hargrave, had first learned of her Aunt Sarah's contribution to Civil Rights history when Krystal asked her grandmother for suggestions for a school project on heroes, and the grandmother told her about Aunt Sarah. I thought this would be a wonderful way to frame a book for kids on this topic, to tell the story through Krystal's experience.

To find out more about this episode in Civil Rights history, I searched through libraries and on the Internet. Again I was surprised: There were few books or articles that mentioned the role these two women played in the Civil Rights Movement. I set out to help correct that oversight by writing this book for young people.

Mrs. Evans's story is an especially important one for young people because it illustrates several important lessons for youth today: that it's not just famous people who make history, that in times of trouble ordinary people can step up and accomplish remarkable things. Also, this story shows that change is a step-by-step process, with many small contributions occurring along the way, all helping to bring about big shifts in attitudes and laws.

Mrs. Evans's actions definitely played an important role in ending the Jim Crow era. This was a shameful period in U.S. history that started in the final years of the nineteenth century when Southern states began passing unfair laws to discriminate against African Americans. The laws were nicknamed "Jim Crow" after an insulting name for black people that some whites used back then. The name became popular just before the Civil War from a white minstrel show performer who pretended to be black and did a silly "Jim Crow" dance to make fun of African Americans. But there was nothing funny about Jim Crow laws. Some made it hard for Southern blacks to vote. Others prevented blacks from going to schools, restaurants, hospitals, or libraries with whites. Jim Crow laws also meant blacks could not sit in the same section of a bus or in the same train cars as whites.

People were beaten and killed for challenging Jim Crow laws. Even so, brave individuals stood up for their rights. One of the first who did so was Homer A. Plessy, arrested in 1892 for not leaving an all-white car on a Louisiana train. He appealed his arrest to the U.S. Supreme Court.

Unfortunately, the Supreme Court decided in 1896 that it was OK for Homer Plessy to have been arrested, that it was all right to have "separate but equal" services for blacks and whites.

Over the years, others continued to challenge those unfair laws. Gradually judges came to realize that segregating the races wasn't right. A big step forward came in 1946 when a woman named Irene Morgan protested all the way to the U.S. Supreme Court about her arrest in Virginia for not sitting in the back of an interstate (state-to-state) bus. The Supreme Court agreed with her and struck down the Virginia law that called for seating by race in state-to-state travel.

However, this decision dealt only with *laws* and not with *rules* a bus company might make. Many interstate bus companies used this loophole to set unfair rules and kept discriminating against blacks. Then Sarah Keys filed a complaint with the ICC challenging her 1952 arrest for not moving to the back of an interstate bus in North Carolina. The ICC decided in 1955 that Sarah Keys had been wrongfully arrested. The ICC actually announced decisions in two cases on the same day, November 25, 1955: one in the Sarah Keys case and the other in a similar case concerning train travel filed by the NAACP. In these twin rulings, the ICC said that blacks traveling state-to-state could no longer be discriminated against either by laws *or* by company rules. Amazingly, "… most rail and bus lines obeyed that command," notes Catherine Barnes in her book *JOURNEY FROM JIM CROW: THE DESEGREGATION OF SOUTHERN TRANSIT.* Those 1955 ICC rulings, combined with the 1954 Supreme Court *Brown v. Board of Education* decision against school segregation, meant the Jim Crow era was crumbling.

A week after the ICC announced its Sarah Keys decision, Rosa Parks led the way in ending discrimination in *local* buses by refusing to move to the back of a local bus in Montgomery, Alabama. One of the leaders of the Montgomery bus boycott and protests that followed her arrest was a young minister making his first appearance as a Civil Rights leader, the Reverend Martin Luther King, Jr. The U.S. Supreme Court soon ruled in their favor. However, some transportation companies in the South refused to obey either the ICC or the Supreme Court. More protests followed, including those of the Freedom Riders, groups of young people who in 1961 boarded buses throughout the South and were arrested and beaten while protesting the remaining discriminatory transportation practices. This led to U.S. Attorney General Robert Kennedy in 1961 putting pressure on the ICC to enforce vigorously the kinds of principles set forth in its 1955 *Sarah Keys v. Carolina Coach Company* ruling. New ICC rulings issued in 1961 finally ended the Jim Crow era in transportation.

After her ICC victory in 1955, Sarah Keys, who had earned her cosmetology license by then, worked as a hair stylist and beauty consultant in Brooklyn until she retired in the 1980s. In 1958, she married George Evans, who for many years was her partner in a beauty salon business and later went back to college to become a counselor and therapist. She had no children of her own but has been an enthusiastic aunt to her many nieces and nephews. Over the years, several other of her nieces besides Krystal have done projects for school about the brave contribution their Aunt Sarah made to Civil Rights history.

Sarah and George Evans, on their wedding day in 1958.

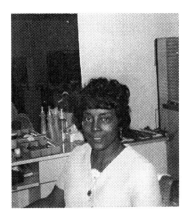

Sarah at the beauty salon in Brooklyn, New York, that she and her husband owned.

Both Sarah Keys Evans and her lawyer, Dovey Roundtree, have received recognition from many groups, including having a small exhibit about them placed on display in 1999 at the Women In Military Service For America Memorial, located at the entrance to Arlington National Cemetery, just outside of Washington, D.C. In 2006, Mrs. Evans received a Trailblazer Award from the United States Department of Justice, presented by Roslynn R. Mauskopf, U.S. Attorney for the Eastern District of New York, at a special ceremony in the U.S. Attorney's office in Brooklyn, New York.

Sarah in February 2006 when she received a Trailblazer Award from the United States Department of Justice, presented in Brooklyn, New York, by Roslynn R. Mauskopf, U.S. Attorney for the Eastern District of New York.

Congressman Major R. Owens

United States House of Representatives
Eleventh Congressional District, Brooklyn, New York

Proclamation
Saluting and Commending

Sarah Keys Evans

Whereas, Sarah Keys Evans, joined the Women's Army Corps (WAC) in 1951, assigned to Fort Dix in New Jersey as an information clerk and receptionist; and,

Whereas, Sarah Keys Evans in 1952, while taking furlough, took a stand and refused to give up her seat and move to the back of the bus; and,

Whereas, Sarah Keys Evans fought this injustice until 1955 when, the Interstate Commerce Commissioner ruled that black passengers who paid the same amount as white passengers must receive the same service; and,

Whereas, Sarah Keys Evans through her actions in 1952, challenged segregation, resulting in a key civil rights decision; and,

Whereas, Sarah Keys, after her discharge from the service in 1953, made her home in Brooklyn, New York where, in 1958, she married George Evans; and,

Whereas, Sarah Keys fought her battle against segregation and humiliations as a matter of moral decency and learned first hand about mental and physical fear thus exemplifying extraordinary courage worthy of being saluted as a POINT-OF-LIGHT; therefore,

Be It Resolved, that I on behalf of the citizens of the Eleventh Congressional District of Brooklyn, New York do hereby salute and commend Sarah Keys Evans in recognition of her outstanding accomplishment in the history of the Civil Rights Movement.

Given my hand and seal this twenty-sixth day of March, Two Thousand and Six.

Major R. Owens
Member of Congress

A proclamation issued in March 2006 by Representative Major R. Owens, United States House of Representatives, saluting Sarah Keys Evans for "her extraordinary courage" and "her outstanding accomplishment in the history of the Civil Rights Movement."

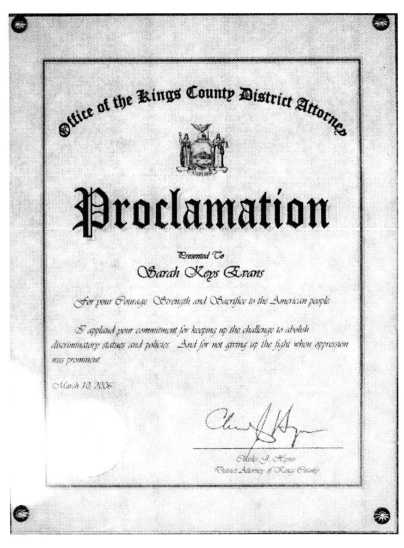

A proclamation issued in March 2006 by
District Attorney Charles Hynes, Kings County, New York,
honoring Sarah Keys Evans for her
"commitment for keeping up the challenge to abolish
discriminatory ... policies and for not giving up the fight
when oppression was prominent."

References

Barnes, Catherine. *Journey From Jim Crow: The Desegregation of Southern Transit.* New York: Columbia University Press, 1983.

Davis, Ronald L. F. *Creating Jim Crow: In Depth Essay.* www.jimcrowhistory.org/home.htm

McCabe, Katie. "She Had a Dream." *Washingtonian Magazine,* March 2002.

Palmore, Joseph R. *The Not-So-Strange Career of Interstate Jim Crow: Race, Transportation, and the Dormant Commerce Clause, 1878–1946.* Virginia Law Review: November, 1997.

http://www.womensmemorial.org/historyandcollections/collections/exhibitpages/afamkoreaexhibit/afamkeys.html

White, Walter. *How Far the Promised Land?* New York: The Viking Press, 1955.

NOTE: The ICC was disbanded in 1995; its functions were taken over by other parts of the Department of Transportation.

Sarah Keys Evans, November 2005.

978-0-595-41761-2
0-595-41761-2

Breinigsville, PA USA
26 January 2011
254220BV00002B/10/A